I0470398

# The Handy Guide For Your iPhone
## iPhone XS – XS Max

# Matthew Stone

# Table of Contents

# Introduction

The iPhone is a product that is manufactured and distributed by the multinational technology corporation, Apple, Inc. This company was founded by Steve Jobs, the company's chairman and CEO, the personal computing pioneer Steve "Woz" Wozniak, and their administrative overseer Ronald Wayne, who ended up selling his 10% share in this new company for a total of $800

USD. Only a year later, he also accepted another $1500 USD to forfeit any potential claims to the newly incorporated entity in the future, for only$2300 USD in total. These men brought the company to life in 1976 in order to sell Wozniak's new personal computer, the Apple I. Later on, they began to design, produce, and sell various electronic products and online services in the global market.

These electronics include the iOS line of devices such as iPod portable media player, iPhone smartphones, and iPad tablet computers. They also sold other products, like the Macintosh personal computer, which utilized the Mac Operating System designed by Apple, the Apple TV, and the HomePod smart speaker.

Apple's impressive list of online services consists of useful tools such as the iCloud, iTunes, Apple Music, the iOS App Store, and the Mac App Store. They also provide many more useful products, such as the operating systems MacOS, iOS, and WatchOS, iLife creativity, the web browser Safari, Xcode, Final Cut Pro, and Logic Pro.

Apple was one of the largest earning firms during the fiscal year of 2017 and owned up to $229 billion at the time. They were the third largest seller on a global level, based on the sales of iOS devices alone. Apple maintains and manages around 504 retail stores in 24 major countries, and has the honor of being the employer of 123,000 workers as of 2018. With all of this in mind, it isn't at all surprising that the company is valued at around $1 trillion and has managed to become such a large name in and outside of its industry. The business community, of course, had had quite a large handful of significant comments about the company's carbon footprint, anti-competitive behavior, questionable labor practices, and the actual origin of their raw materials. Apple has, of course, managed to push past these difficulties, though. They have worked hard to gain the trust of their customers and believe very strongly in the concept of brand loyalty.

Over 1 billion individual devices from Apple are being used and adored around the world, and with the interconnectedness and cross-functionality across Apple's various products, this number is constantly increasing at alarming rates.

In an interview from March 2014, the designer of Apple, Inc. referred to the iPhone as "the epitome of high-quality product development". According to him, iPhones are comparatively more expensive than devices from other brands due to the extensive effort and the resources that are utilized in their making. When the company began to manufacture the iPhone, active decisions were made in order to keep their design and properties separate and unique from similar, competing models. Now, there have been several models launched, each with an increased and improved sense of uniqueness and quality, and all of which have seemed to take the world by storm. Recently, Apple Inc.

Has released new versions of the iPhone with even more unique features and higher levels of power and precision. These are the successors to the iPhone X, referred to as the iPhone XS, its larger, upgraded edition called the iPhone XS Max, and the slightly simpler model, which has been named the iPhone XR.

This book intends to illuminate the features of these new devices and their operating system, iOS 12, in great detail. It will include their specifications, pros and cons, tips and tricks to help you use them to their best and fullest capacity, and a clear and differential analysis of the latest products in comparison to their ancestors. By the end, you should possess all of the tools necessary to do so and properly utilize all of the applications and other features available to you on your new iPhone XS, XS Max, or XR.

# Chapter 1: Main iPhone Features

The iPhone is special because it seems to have its own completely separate market from similar devices. This is because of the many useful and unique features available exclusively on iPhones. Listed below are all of the Primary features of the iPhone and brief guides on how to use them properly and to their full extent.

**Phone:**

The first feature will, of course, be the phone function itself. It contains innovative features, like the visual voicemail, which will display voicemails as text to be read, as opposed to the audio format which needs to be listened to. The Phone application will allow you to make calls and view your voicemails. The Phone application's features will be listed below;

- Keypad: Lets you dial numbers manually to call or add to contacts.

- Recents: Lists your recent calls and allows you to redial.

- Contacts: Lists all of your saved contacts and lets you add new ones.

- Favorites: Lists your favorited contacts for easier access.

- Voicemail: Allows you to listen to view and listen to voicemails. Visual Voicemail is an option, as well.

**Multi-touch Screen:**

While the older iPhone models had a 3.5-inch display, the new iPhone X and XS have a 5.8-inch OLED with a "super retina" display that has a higher pixel count and an impressive upgrade in its dynamic range over the previous models, with an astonishing 60% increase. The multi-touch screen, of course, incorporates a new "Multi-touch" technology. This new feature enables the utilization of multiple points of contact to perform new and useful functions on the touch screen that weren't possible before.

Some of the most discussed features of the iPhone are due to the multi-touch capabilities of the new devices, such as the ability to double tap on the device's screen in order to enlarge the image by zooming in, or by "pinching", which can be done by placing two fingers on the screen and moving them closer together or further apart on the screen in order to zoom in and out of a photograph or webpage. They also have a "3D Touch", which allows you to use varying degrees of pressure and sensitivity when touching the screen in order to see content previews, actions, and contextual menus.

This setting can be enabled in the "General settings" menu, under "accessibility", and then "3D Touch".

## Web Browsing:

iPhones offer a complete and comprehensive browsing experience for their users. Unlike Android phones that use dumbed-down, overly-simplistic "mobile" versions of websites, the iPhone's browsers provide a better and more full interface, which is more akin to a traditional "desktop" browser.

## Email:

iPhones, much like all smartphones, consist of a robust email experience that can conveniently sync to corporate email servers running Exchange. They contain all of the standard email features that are offered by your carrier, and can even use multiple accounts. These accounts can be managed in the device's "Passwords & Accounts" settings.

## Calendar:

In addition to functioning as a phone, the iPhone has the ability to manage your personal information with the help of incredibly handy features such as the address book, weather updates, stock management, and the calendar. The calendar can, of course, be accessed and managed via the "Calendar" application. Through it, you can schedule events and appointments for any point in the future. This is a great way to stay organized and minimize confusion in daily life.

## Clock:

The "Clock" application is also useful for scheduling and, obviously, keeping track of time. There are several functions within the application that can be useful for many day- to-day tasks:

- World Clock: Can keep track of multiple timezones, in case you travel or frequently interact with people in or from other timezones.

- Alarm: Another good way to maintain a proper schedule. You can set alarms for certain times, and manage those alarms here.

- Bedtime: If you stick to a consistent sleep schedule, or want to do so, the bedtime function can help you. You can set specific times during which your iPhone will track your sleep patterns. It can also be programmed with "Do Not Disturb", or to have an alarm set when you wish to wake up.

- Stopwatch: The stopwatch will function as a stopwatch. It has stop, start, lap, and reset functions, for timing the amount of time certain tasks take.

- Timer: Exactly like a timer, this function will count down from a set time. You can start, stop, and reset the timer as well.

**Audio/Video Playback:**

The size of the various models of iOS devices, such as the iPod and iPhone also changed over time. What has been a reliable constant, however, is the exceptional quality of these devices' hardware, which had made the experience of both audio and video based content consumption all the more mesmerizing. You can use services such as the iTunes store or YouTube to easily find media, and consume it in stunning quality.

## Cameras:

One of the more major changes made in recent iPhone models, such as the XS, XS Max, and XR are the cameras. While the rear-facing camera still shoots in higher resolution than the front one, these models have enclosed two cameras on each side, as opposed to only one. This allows for depth perception, which produces even higher-quality photos and videos, in addition to the camera's other features and uses like specialized editing, 3D photos, FaceTime, and Animoji.

## Applications:

Apple has its own marketplace for applications that can be used for just about anything that Apple devices can be used for, from tools like flashlights, compasses, and gyroscopes to games like Fruit Ninja, Flappy Bird, and Angry Birds. Some of these applications can require payment to be used, but often there are free versions with ads embedded to help the developers support themselves if they choose to release these free applications. This marketplace is called the Apple App Store, and its third-party programs help to add even more versatility and value to these already incredibly flexible devices. Once an Application is installed, it will be placed on the home screen for easy access.

## Home Screen:

The iPhone has a very user-friendly interface that allows its users to rearrange their application icons to their preference. The user can create folders and group icons accordingly, or leave applications outside on the home screen if they so choose. This is where new applications downloaded from the App Store will go by default. You can press and hold on an icon to bring up options for that application, if you want to uninstall or move it.

**Home Button:**

The home button is placed at the bottom center of the phone and is used to wake the phone and open the App Switcher, which allows you to view open applications and close them, if you choose. In recent models of the iPhone, this button has been removed. The home button is now a part of the multi-touch screen as a digital button on the bottom of your iPhone XS, XS Max, or XR's display.

**Hold Button:**

The "Hold Button" can be located on the right side of your device, toward the top of the screen. It is a small, oblong button that you can feel by sliding your finger along the device's side. The primary function of this button, which you will end up using the most, is to lock and unlock the screen and put the device to sleep or wake it up. It is also used to restart the phone and power it down completely. This can be done by holding it for several seconds until a "power off" slider appears on the device's display.

**Volume Buttons:**

The device's volume control buttons can be located on the device's left side, across from the hold button. There are two volume buttons, one up and one down. They are used to control the device's volume settings, including the ringer, videos, and music players.

**Ringer Switch:**

Located directly over the volume buttons, near the top of your device on the left side, is a small, oblong switch. This switch will allow the user to place their device in "silent mode" in order to prevent their device from ringing audibly when it receives calls. If this switch is in the red position, this means it is on, and your device won't ring audibly. To turn it off, simply flip the switch again.

## Dock Connector:

The more recent iPhone models have added wireless charging as a new feature. This capability is present in the XS and XS Max iPhone models, but is unfortunately absent in the XR. There is, however, still a dock port for lightning connectors provided on the bottom side of the device. This is provided for the purpose of charging, with the lightning cable. It can also be used for data transfer, and can be plugged into a computer to sync with iTunes and move files from one device to the other. There are also many accessories, such as headphones, that can be used through this port as well.

## Sync:

As soon as the iPhone is activated for the first time, the user is instructed to input their details to the device. This includes your Apple ID, which enables the phone to sync personal data such as the calendar and contacts, if they were previously backed up to the iCloud. It is also recommended that users periodically back up their device with iTunes, as well. These methods can be helpful in preventing data loss in the case of accidental damage or if the device has been lost or stolen. This can be done over the iCloud from the settings, under [Your Name], in the "iCloud" submenu. If you manually back up your device to the iCloud, however, it will not automatically back up as scheduled for 24 hours afterward. This can be important to note if you have automatic backups scheduled.

## Reset and Restore:

The iTunes application can also be used to reset your iPhone to its factory settings and to restore content from a previous backup when issues arise that cause your device to become unusable, and the only way to rectify these issues is to erase the device's contents. This can happen if the device is sent to recovery mode. If your device becomes unusable, you might have to put it into recovery mode in order to restore it from an iTunes backup. This can be done by pressing the up volume button, then the down button, and then pressing the lock button and holding it until your device displays the apple logo on its screen. You will then be able to plug your device into your windows or Mac computer with iTunes and restore it from an old backup by following the prompts provided from the iTunes program.

# Chapter 2: Novelties and Unique Features

## Super Retina Display:

The new iPhone models consist of a 5.8-inch OLED screen display, similar to iPhone X. They also, however, contain an upgraded component in the screen, which is referred to as the "Super Retina Display". This new display style has a much improved dynamic range over the previous model. It is able to pack more pixels as well, and overall carries a much higher resolution, for smoother images and a brighter display. The new iPhone's Super Retina Display sets the record for the largest display of its type, containing approximately 3.3 million pixels.

## Face Recognition:

A product of the dual-camera setup's depth perception, face recognition is one of the amazing and novel features that make the iPhone so secure. This feature allows a user to use their face to unlock their device by placing their face in front of the cameras.

Although this feature is also present in some newer Samsung models, the iPhone's facial recognition technology is unique in that it used the 3D capabilities of the dual cameras in order to get a more accurate image of the user's face. This allows for a more accurate reading, which not only makes it easier for the user to use, but also improves the overall security of the device. Apple takes great pride in their many advanced security features and challenges that this facial recognition lock cannot be breached even by professionally-made face masks.

## Animoji:

As all companies are developing their own versions of emojis, Apple has decided to take that concept a step further with emojis that are able to work in cooperation with facial recognition software in a fun and immersive way. The facial recognition software captures your image and matches it with the emoji that you are using in order to animate the image and allow you even more creativity than ever. These "animated emojis" are cleverly referred to as "Animoji". If you record a short clip of your face making an expression, gesturing your head, or talking, the animoji will mimic those actions with surprising precision and allow you to record these actions with the animoji filter to send to whoever you may wish to send them to.

## Wireless Charging:

The iPhone 8, the 8 Plus, and the iPhone X were the first iPhone models that were designed and manufactured with wireless charging capabilities. The method of wireless charging chosen by Apple can be slow at times, but with newer, more recent models, the wireless charging capabilities have seen significant improvement which will only grow more with time and progress. While the iPhone XS and XS Max are capable of charging wirelessly, the iPhone XR does not possess this incredibly useful and convenient technology.

## A12 Bionic Processor:

The A12 Bionic processor in the new iPhone is one of the fastest chips on the planet. This 7 nanometer-wide chip contains 6.7 billion transistors. It also possesses and an 8- core devoted engine with machine learning capabilities to evaluate data sent from a neural network in order for it to decide if the processes should be carried out through that neural engine or not. The A12 Bionic processor uses less energy and can perform 5 trillion operations per second, giving it the ability to open apps 30 times faster than previous iPhones

## Cameras:

iPhones have always had amazing quality in their cameras, especially compared to competing devices. With wide-angle camera lens with a resolution of 12 megapixels, and another secondary camera for things like capturing 3D images and registering depth perception, the new iPhone models' cameras offer massive upgrades compared to the ones featured in older devices, such as the iPhone 7 Plus, the first model to feature a telescoping lens. You can also see noticeably smoother photos and videos, better low- light photograph quality, and more. Additionally, with the newer "True Depth" camera in the front-side, you will be able to take better portrait-style photos, thanks to a feature that was also new to the 7 Plus, which can create a "Bokeh" effect with improved focusing technology that blurs the background slightly in order to highlight the foreground more, in order to help create a more professional-looking photo. You can also adjust the photo depth with the depth slider. The XS and XS Max can both still support a vertical configuration camera with improved tone LED flash accompanied by an advanced flicker system in its 12-megapixel telephoto lens camera. The front-facing camera has 2 times faster sensors with improved red-eye reduction, along with detailed segmentation to further boost the quality of all of your photos and videos.

**Smart HDR:**

In the XS model, a smart HDRA is powered by the same A12 chip that allows the phone's image signal processor and neural engine to chain multiple pictures into one by using techniques like zero shutter lag and highlight, and result in better picture quality. The camera is now also able to take improved photos, make videos with greater highlight structure in low-light conditions.

**Apple Bookstore:**

The Apple Bookstore is handy when looking for new books to read, or old ones you liked. It considers information such as the authors, genres, and topics in order to make it easier than ever to find interesting reading material. Within the application, you can easily shuffle between books you may be reading quickly, without needing to close one and open the other manually. You can also add books to your wishlist to help you keep track of the ones you want to read next, and purchase them with ease.

**Apple Music:**

Apple Music is a fun and efficient way of listening to the music you like. The iPhone provides the Apple Music application, which helps you to personalize your music according to your own taste. You can find specific songs by searching by the song title, artist, album, or even the lyrics. Apple Music will also recommend your top songs from daily charts and your own history.

## Apple News:

For those who like to stay up-to-date with current events, iOS offers the "Apple News" application, which can help you keep track of events as they occur. Apple News can suggest articles based on your own interests, as well, to help you stay informed regarding the topics that interest you. With Apple News, it has become easier than ever to stay informed and find material relevant to specific topics that interest you.

# Chapter 3: Differences Between iPhone Models

As the past decade has gone by, Apple has continuously introduced newer iPhone models that are each better and more advanced than the last one. This chapter will be taking you through the journey of iPhone models up to the current models that have allowed Apple to take its place as one of the world's most high-tech and successful mobile phone manufacturers.

The iPhone 3G didn't have 3G data or GPS, both of which were introduced later on the following year with a second version which also had a better body. Its current battery was 1150 mA with a Voltage of 3.7 V, and it consisted of Bluetooth 2.0 EDR with a rear camera of 1.9 megapixels, surely nowhere near the latest iPhone models. Its core design was ARM1176 x 1 with a CPU speed of 412 MHz and it had 128 MB RAM, whereas the new latest

RAM ranges to 525 GB. In another year, Apple released the iPhone 3GS where S meant "speed." Its battery was better as compared to the previous iPhone with 1219mA. It has a 3.1 rear camera. The core design of this phone was ARM Cortex-A8 x 1 with a CPU speed of 620 MHz and 256 MB of RAM.

After this came the iPhone 4 which looked better than all the previous phones. The front camera was first introduced in the iPhone 4, and took its popularity to a whole new level. It had a better battery of 1419mA and rear camera of 5.2 megapixels, whereas the front camera was 0.3 megapixels. Its core design was ARM Cortex-A8 x 1 with a CPU

Speed of 800 MHz but their RAM and storage space was similar to the previous iPhones. The iPhone 4s didn't have many changes in comparison to its predecessor. One new feature that the iPhone 4s introduced was the entry of Siri and a high-resolution camera, which was able to record play a 1080pHD videos.

The iPhone 5 came with bigger screen displays due to consumer demand. These phones were a quarter inch taller than their predecessors. The width was kept similar. This phone was not user-friendly because of its length, and could not support easy usage with a hand, but the iPhone 5 was one of the first iPhones to support LTE (wireless internet communication technology). It was also one of the first phones to use the new lightning port for charging and data transfer that had been developed by Apple, as opposed to their older, wider 30-pin connectors that were present in previous versions of the iPhone and iPod. It had a 1GB RAM and a 64GB storage space with an 8 megapixels rear camera and a 1.2 megapixels front camera. In the iPhone 5S, the main change was the introduction of the Touch ID fingerprint scanner. Previously, this feature was used only for App Stores and authentic downloads but, in later iPhones, new security additions have been made, such as face recognition. They had introduced the color gold for the first time through this iPhone. The iPhone 5c was comparatively cheaper than the 5S and was the only model since the iPhone 3GS to have a plastic body and a selection of different colors. At $499, it was $200 cheaper than iPhone 5S but was still considered expensive in comparison to other mid-level smartphones. In short, Apple failed to produce a budget friendly smartphone in 2015.

The iPhone 6 and 6 Plus had a far better design than the awkwardly elongated design of their predecessor. Both models were very similar in features. The significant external difference being that of screen size with the 6 Plus consisting of a larger screen. The only internal difference was the presence of an optical image stabilizer in the iPhone 6 Plus that allowed the Apps to be displayed in landscape mode in larger devices. These were also the first Apple phones to feature the much celebrated Apple Pay. After this came the famous iPhone 6S which introduced a new feature called "3D Touch." Also known as 'pressure touch' users could, for the first time, carry out different tasks by pressing the screen harder. The iPhone 6S was the first model to be launched in rose gold; the most popular skin of all time. The iPhone SE, on the other hand, is one of the smallest phones that Apple developed. It is an attempt for a budget-friendly smartphone for emerging markets. It has the exterior of iPhone 5S i.e. a plastic body and small screen size of just 4 inches but comes with all the powerful features of the iPhone 6S.

With the launch of iPhone 7 and 7 Plus, Apple again launched two models at the same time with different screen sizes and price points. The iPhone 7 and 7 Plus were the first iPhones to come without a headphone jack. They were also the first iPhones that did not have a physical home button and also the first iPhones that were waterproof. Unlike the iPhone 7, the iPhone 7 Plus consisted of a double-rear camera which could measure depth, resulting in quite impressive portrait shots.

Apple released the new iPhone 8 and 8 Plus on September 12, 2017. These new models were presented as the most recent in the line of upgrades to Apple's iOS Devices. They possessed better, more efficient processors and many other features designed to maximize the iPhone's potential and effectiveness. The iPhone 8 had upgraded camera hardware and better displays with improved resolution as well, for even higher-quality visual content creation and consumption. Of course, they also possessed the new wireless charging technology that Apple had developed, which was a somewhat controversial topic at the time but ultimately served to improve the overall quality of iPhone use and made them easier and more enjoyable to use. Apple had also revealed the iPhone X, which altered the iPhone's hardware even further. The iPhone X introduced a new feature designed to streamline the use of Apple's devices moving forward, by removing the home button that was present in previous models and replaced them with the new digital home indicator bar. They also added new gesture technology, wireless charging capabilities, and facial recognition software.

Apple finally introduced the successors to the iPhone X on September 12, 2018. These new models were referred to as the iPhone XS, XS Max, and XR. The iPhone XS and XS Max featured new "Super Retina" displays as well as a new and improved dual-camera system. This new camera technology allowed for, as with many of the iPhone's previous models, higher-quality photos and videos. Other features include the first chip to be included in a mobile computing device of seven nanometers and another new feature in the A12 Bionic chip, with access to a new neural engine. It was also given faster and more accurate FaceID features, improved stereo sound output range, and the introduction of the iPhone's new Dual SIM capabilities, which allowed for two SIM cards within a single device. The iPhone XR comes with the most impressive smartphone LCD to date, containing a new 6.1-inch Liquid Retina display, the new A12 Bionic chip, and the True Depth dual-camera system that allows for three-dimensional images and the capacity for depth perception for higher-quality photos and videos.

# Chapter 4: iPhone XS

The newer model of iPhone , the iPhone XS, is slightly smaller than its predecessor, the iPhone X. It does, however, have many new features and upgrades over the older model that will be described in this chapter.

**Price per Capacity:**

The price of this iPhone depends on its capacity. It's $999 for the 64GB, $1,149 for the 256GB or $1,349 for the 512GB.

**Colors:**

The iPhone XS is available in a stainless-steel body that comes in three colors: space grey, gold, and silver.

## Screen/Display:

The iPhone XS possesses a decently-sized diagonal 5.8 inches in a 458 pixel-per-inch OLED "Super Retina" HDR display, whereas the iPhone 8 Plus only had a total screen size of 5.5 inches. The iPhone XS does have slightly less total volume in its screen, however, as it is also slightly thinner as well.

## Height:

The iPhone XS has a height of 5.65 inches, or 143.6 mm.

## Weight:

It is 6.24 ounces (177 grams) heavy.

## Depth:

The depth of iPhone XS is 0.30-inch (7.7 mm).

## Width:

The width of iPhone XS is 2.79-inches (70.9 mm).

## Splash Water and Dust Resistant:

The iPhone XS is resistant to both water and dust. It is waterproof and has been estimated to be able to last for approximately 30 minutes at a depth of up to 2 meters when fully submerged in water.

## Bionic Chip:

This new chip contains artificial intelligence software that reaches entirely new tiers of efficiency and excellence. The A12 Bionic Chip, paired with a next-generation neural engine, to deliver impressive results. For example, it provides powerful real-time machine learning that produces amazing results for gaming, photos, augmented reality, etc. This chip has increased the speed of functions by 15% as compared to the A11 Bionic chip. It also allows the device an additional 50% higher efficient battery consumption rate over the a11 model. The A12 Bionic chip delivers a 50% faster graphics performance. Apple designed this new neural engine to allow its devices to learn from its users based on their patterns and preferences in order to make accurate predictions for things like text corrections and product advertisements that might interest their users based on this information. All of this new technology helps to make the iPhone XS, XS Max, and XR that much more capable and efficient to maximize their users' satisfaction.

## Camera:

It consists of Smart HDR that encapsulates multiple technologies inside it. It encompasses faster sensors, an enhanced ISP, and advanced algorithms. Smart HDR is used to enhance the quality of photos through better highlight and shadow. The new iPhones have even more effective technology that allow for better effects, like the Bokeh, or background blur effect, for better quality portrait Photos. The camera produces a new "True Depth" depth map to keep the background blurred while the user is in focus helping to deliver enhanced portrait mode photos. This new iPhone's camera's sensors use new rendering technology and allow more thorough light sensors within the camera's hardware in order to help improve the quality of any photos you might take in low light conditions, as well as the photos you take in normal conditions as well. These new sensors combine with a new feature that allows for effectively no shutter-lag to erase any motion-blur in your photos and create more prominent highlights and detailed shadows as well. The iPhone XS can also record videos with amazing quality with the help of its new low light filters at a consistent rate of 30 frames per second, and can even maintain dual-channel audio recording and playback.

### Facial Landmarking:

Once a face is detected, facial landmarking allows the iPhone camera to adjust the portrait lightning as per the subject in focus.

### Mapping the Depth:

The iPhone has the ability to keep the subject and the background separate due to the advanced neural engine combined with advanced depth engine of ISP.

Moreover, Portrait mode captures depth information that lets you adjust the depth of field and add creative Portrait Lighting effects. It consists of twin 12-megapixel rear- facing cameras with wide angle lenses. In addition, it has a 7MP True Depth front camera with a $f/2.2$ wide-angle lens.

### Power and Battery:

The battery of iPhone XS Lasts up to 30 minutes longer than the iPhone X. It has a built-in rechargeable lithium-ion battery inside it. It is supported by wireless charging (works with Qi chargers), and it can also be charged through a USB to a computer system or power adapter.

### Talk Time (Wireless):

After one full charge, the talk time can last up to 20 hours.

### Internet Use:

It can support up to 12 hours of continuous internet use from a full charge.

**Video Playback (Wireless):**

The user can easily play videos up to 14 hours after a full charge.

**Audio Playback (Wireless):**

It provides the facility of up to 60 hours of audio playback after a full charge.

**Fast-Charge Capable:**

It takes the iPhone XS, only 30 minutes to charge 50%.

**Sensors:**

The iPhone XS consists of three-axis gyro, Accelerometer, Proximity sensor, Ambient light sensor, and Barometer.

**SIM Card:**

It has a Dual SIM (nano-SIM and eSIM) which is not compatible with existing micro- SIM cards

**Connector:**

It consists of a Lightning charging port.

**Audio Calling:**

You can initiate audio calls over WiFi or cellular to any FaceTime audio-enabled device.

**Secure Authentication:**

It uses Face identification for a higher level of personal security which is improved by the True Depth camera's 3d image capture capabilities for depth perception and more accurate readings of your face for security purposes.

# Chapter 5: iPhone XS Max

If you are into watching movies, taking photos, recording videos, or doing anything involving the screen, then the iPhone XS Max is the one for you. This chapter will be similar to the last, and will list details and features of the iPhone XS Max.

**Price per Capacity:**

Obviously, the iPhone XS Max is a little different than the XS. It is a little bit larger and beefier, and as such, the prices are also a bit higher. The price of this iPhone depends on the capacity, though, as with the standard XS model. The XS Max is a very simple and clean $100 increase in price over the XS, with prices listed at $1099 for the 64GB, $1,249 for the 256GB, and an impressive $1,449 for the 512GB.

**Colors:**

The iPhone XS is available in a stainless-steel body that comes in three colors, just as with the iPhone XS. These color options are space grey, gold, and stainless steel silver.

**Screen/Display:**

With an even more astonishing 19.5:9 aspect ratio and a 6.5-inch diagonal True Tone "Super Retina" 458 pixels-per-inch display and an objective screen resolution of 2688 x 1242 pixels, the iPhone XS steps it up just a bit with the same type of display as the XS, but slightly larger overall.

**Height:**

The iPhone XS Max has a height of 6.2 inches, or 157.5 mm.

**Depth:**

The depth of iPhone XS Max is the same as the standard XS, at 0.30-inch (7.7 mm).

**Width:**

The width of iPhone XS Max is 3.05-inches (77.4).

**Weight:**

The iPhone XS Max weighs in at 7.34 ounces, or 208 grams.

**Splash Water and Dust Resistant:**

The iPhone XS Max, just like the XS, resistant to both water and dust. It is waterproof and has been estimated to be able to last for approximately 30 minutes at a depth of up to 2 meters when fully submerged in water.

**Bionic Chip:**

This new chip contains artificial intelligence software that reaches entirely new tiers of efficiency and excellence. The A12 Bionic Chip, paired with a next-generation neural engine, to deliver impressive results. For example, it provides powerful real-time machine learning that produces amazing results for gaming, photos, augmented reality, etc. This chip has increased the speed of functions by 15% as compared to the A11 Bionic chip. It also allows the device an additional 50% higher efficient battery consumption rate over the a11 model. The A12 Bionic chip delivers a 50% faster graphics performance. Apple designed this new neural engine to allow its devices to learn from its users based on their patterns and preferences in order to make accurate predictions for things like text corrections and product advertisements that might interest their users based on this information. All of this new technology helps to make the iPhone XS, XS Max, and XR that much more capable and efficient to maximize their users' satisfaction.

**Camera:**

It consists of Smart HDR that encapsulates multiple technologies inside it. It encompasses faster sensors, an enhanced ISP, and advanced algorithms. Smart HDR is used to enhance the quality of photos through better highlight and shadow. The new iPhones have even more effective technology that allow for better effects, like the Bokeh, or background blur effect, for better quality portrait Photos. The camera produces a new "True Depth" depth map to keep the background blurred while the user is in focus helping to deliver enhanced portrait mode photos. This new iPhone's camera's sensors use new rendering technology and allow more thorough light sensors within the camera's hardware in order to help improve the quality of any photos you might take in low light conditions, as well as the photos you take in normal conditions as well. These new sensors combine with a new feature that allows for effectively no shutter-lag to erase any motion-blur in your photos and create more prominent highlights and detailed shadows as well. The iPhone XS can also record videos with amazing quality with the help of its new low light filters at a consistent rate of 30 frames per second, and can even maintain dual-channel audio recording and playback.

**Facial Landmarking:**

Once a face is detected, facial landmarking allows the iPhone camera to adjust the portrait lightning as per the subject in focus.

**Mapping the Depth:**

The iPhone has the ability to keep the subject and the background separate due to the advanced neural engine combined with advanced depth engine of ISP.

Moreover, Portrait mode captures depth information that lets you adjust the depth of field and add creative Portrait Lighting effects. It consists of twin 12-megapixel rear- facing cameras with wide angle lenses. In addition, it has a 7MP True Depth front camera with a $f/2.2$ wide-angle lens.

**Power and Battery:**

The battery of iPhone XS Max Lasts up to 90 minutes longer than the iPhone X. It is supported by wireless charging (works with Qi chargers), and it can also be charged through a USB to a computer system or power adapter.

**Talk Time (Wireless):**

After one full charge, the talk time can last for as long as 25 hours.

**Internet Use:**

It can handle as many as 13 hours of continuous internet use from a full charge.

**Video Playback (Wireless):**

The user can easily play videos up to 14 hours after a full charge.

**Audio Playback (Wireless):**

It provides the facility of up to 60 hours of audio playback after a full charge.

**Fast-Charge Capable:**

It takes the iPhone XS, only 30 minutes to charge 50%.

**Sensors:**

The iPhone XS consists of three-axis gyro, Accelerometer, Proximity sensor, Ambient light sensor, and Barometer.

**SIM Card:**

It has a Dual SIM (nano-SIM and eSIM) which is not compatible with existing micro- SIM cards

**Connector:**

It consists of a Lightning charging port.

**Audio Calling:**

You can initiate audio calls over WiFi or cellular to any FaceTime audio-enabled device.

**Secure Authentication:**

It uses Face identification for a higher level of personal security which is improved by the True Depth camera's 3d image capture capabilities for depth perception and more accurate readings of your face for security purposes.

# Chapter 6: Tips and Tricks

There are many ways to utilize the iPhone XS, XS Max, and XR to their maximum efficiency, but some of their shortcuts may not immediately intuitive at a glance. Some of the features of these devices aren't necessarily things that you would think to use if you aren't already familiar with them. This isn't to say, of course, that they can't be useful, though. Several of these shortcuts can be extremely helpful in day-to-day life and will let you streamline your experience with your new device. Listed below are some tips and tricks to help you get the most out of your iPhone XS, XS Max, or XR.

**Power Off:**

In order to turn off the phone, or make an emergency call with your iPhone XS, hold the side button and one of the volume buttons at the same time, and then drag to turn off the device, use the Medical ID or make an emergency call.

**Reset:**

Performing a hard reset on the iPhone XS is a little bit more complicated than just turning the device off with the power slider. Luckily, this manual reset method is also fairly simple. You need to press the volume up button on the left side of the device.

Then, press the volume down button directly below. Finally, you will need to press and hold the power button on the right side of the screen for several seconds, until the Apple logo appears on the screen. Once this logo appears, the full reset can take about 20 to 30 seconds.

**Emergency Calls:**

In order to turn off the phone, or make an emergency call with your iPhone XS, hold the side button and one of the volume buttons at the same time, and then drag to turn off the device, use the Medical ID or make an emergency call.

**Medical ID:**

In order to turn off the phone, or make an emergency call with your iPhone XS, hold the side button and one of the volume buttons at the same time, and then drag to turn off the device, use the Medical ID or make an emergency call.

**Tap to Wake iPhone:**

Your device can be set in such a way that it will allow you to tap on the 3-D display in order to wake your phone up. This is a default setting, but you can also enable or disable it manually by going into the Settings App, selecting "General", moving to the "Accessibility" submenu, and tapping "Tap To Wake" to toggle this feature on or off.

**Attention-Aware Features:**

The iPhone XS can be customized in other ways, as well. You can also activate the "Raise to Wake" setting to allow you to wake up your device without tapping on it or swiping it. This can be done by going to the "Display and Brightness" submenu in your device settings, and toggling on or off the "Raise to Wake" option.

**Face ID Lock:**

With the addition of iOS 12, the newer models of the iPhone have a strong 3D facial recognition tool for security which is considered more reliable as compared to fingerprint recognition. Just go into the Settings App, under the "Face ID & Passcode" submenu and follow the instructions. You can also control the apps which use this feature under the "Face ID & Passcode" settings, in "Other Apps".

**Home Indicator Bar:**

In order to go back to the home screen directly from an open application, you will need to use the new Home Indicator Bar at the bottom of the screen on your iPhone. You simply need to swipe up quickly from the bar on the bottom of the screen, and this action will send you to the device's home screen. If you have multiple pages of application icons on your device, this action will return you to the first page.

**App Switcher:**

The App Switcher can be incredibly useful in switching between applications and closing ones that aren't being used. In order to get to the App Switcher, you simply need to swipe left or right from the Home Indicator Bar on the bottom of the screen. Once you do this, all of your open applications will be displayed on the screen. You can scroll among or between applications in order to open a different one, if it is already open, or swipe up or down to close an application as well.

## Control Center:

The Control Center lets you change settings on your device quickly, such as brightness, volume, and Bluetooth connectivity. To get to the Control Center, you will need to start from the top of the screen on the right side, and swipe downward. To dismiss it, you can swipe your finger in the opposite direction, from the bottom to the top. This will dismiss panel for this function. The Control Center has many settings that are embedded by default. These settings include various different "cards", which will be listed below:

The first card contains connectivity settings, which can be accessed in a small window in the upper left-hand corner of the Control center:

- Airplane Mode: Instantly activate or disable connectivity to and from your iPhone.

- Cellular Data: Instantly activate and disable connectivity for applications or services.

- Wi-Fi: Activate or disable WiFi connectivity to your device.

- Bluetooth: activate or disable Bluetooth connectivity in order to connect to or disconnect from Bluetooth capable devices.

- AirDrop: Activate or disable AirDrop to allow you to share media with other Apple products.

- Personal Hotspot: Activate or disable your device's personal hotspot, which broadcasts your cell signal as a wireless internet connection point.

You can also find the Audio card in the control center's top right-hand corner. Press firmly or press and hold to access this card in order to quickly access its full functionality. It can be used to control any audio-based media you may have active, including music, audiobooks, and podcasts. You can tap the radar icon in this window to change the sound source to any compatible and ready audio output device. It will also display individual cards dedicated to any nearby available devices. Simply tap those cards to control that device's audio output as well.

The Control Center also has many settings within it that you can change, and you can even add or remove various features, depending on your preference. To change the Shortcuts available to you on your Control Center screen, you can go to the device's settings menu, and continue on to the "Control Center" submenu. From here, tap on the "Customize" option. From this menu, you can Add features with the + icon, or remove them with the - icon. You can also rearrange these shortcuts with the icons on the right side of each feature that resemble three horizontal lines. The customizable features of the Control Center that can be changed will be listed below:

- Alarm: You can use this card to help you create alarms for yourself.

- Brightness: You can use this card to change the brightness on your device by sliding the bar.

- Calculator: This card pulls up the calculator application, which functions as a standard calculator or a scientific calculator depending on the screen orientation.

- Do Not Disturb: this card will let you turn on do not

disturb mode. You can set a timeframe for this mode or simply turn it on and deactivate it whenever you choose.

- Do Not Disturb While Driving: This card can be turned on to activate do not disturb mode when you are driving, and will send a quick message to anyone attempting to get in touch with you that you are unavailable.

- Guided Access: this card can restrict which applications or services your device is able to access.

- Low Power Mode: toggling this card will activate low power mode in order to preserve battery life.

- Magnifier: this will activate the camera in order to allow you to use your iPhone as a magnifying glass.

- Scan QR Code: This card will pull up the camera application to scan and open the content within a QR code

- Rotation Lock: This setting will prevent your device from switching its screen orientation.

- Silent Mode: place your device in silent mode to avoid hearing the ringer or notification tones.

- Stopwatch: This card will pull up the clock application's stopwatch function.

- Text Size: This card will let you adjust the size of text that appears on the screen.

- Voice Memos: This card will allow you to use your iPhone's microphone to record an audio clip.

- Volume: This card will let you change the volume of auditory output from your device.

Certain cards have even more functionality. You can press deeply or press and hold in order to view more controls for these cards, listed below:

- Accessibility Shortcuts: This card will make it simpler to activate or deactivate accessibility shortcuts.

- Apple TV Remote: This card will make it easier to control any Apple TV related products from your iPhone.

- Camera: This card will open the camera application for easy access to photo and video capturing.

- Flashlight: Activating this card will toggle your iPhone's rear facing LED light to be used as a flashlight with adjustable brightness settings.

- Hearing Aids: This card will allow you to easily pair your iPhone with heading aids for easier accessibility.

- Home: This card lets you easily access the settings for the Home application.

- Night Shift: This card lets you activate the settings for night mode, which filter out the blue light for nighttime consumption.

- Notes: This card will allow you to easily access the note pad application.

- Screen Mirroring: This card allows you to share your screen with available devices.

- Screen Recording: This card will allow you to capture video of your device's display, much like a screenshot image. You can also capture audio with it, if you choose to do so.

- Timer: The timer card will allow you to access the clock application's timer function.

- True Tone: This card will allow you to alter the color and brightness settings of your device's display to best suit your current environment and time of day.

- Wallet: This card will enable you to quickly access your saved payment information for apple pay.

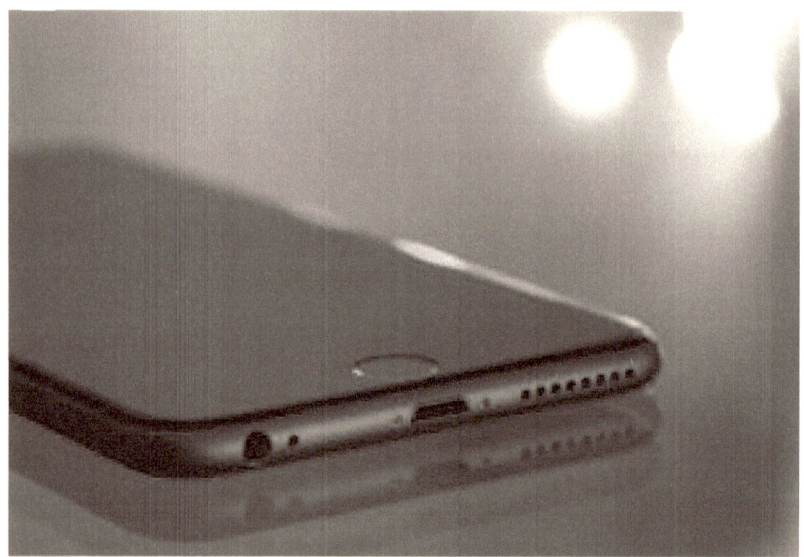

**Notification Bar:**

Swipe from the left edge of the screen towards the right for the notification bar to appear. This screen will display any notifications from apps available at the time, and allow you to either clear the notification, which will remove it from the list, or tap the notification, which will then open the relevant application for you immediately.

## Do Not Disturb:

This is a feature that lets you keep your personal time to yourself without being interrupted by any phone calls or messages. You can easily customize the time period during which you prefer not to be disturbed. After you set the times, the iPhone will automatically go into "Do Not Disturb" mode within those specified timings. When Do Not Disturb is activated, you will see a crescent moon icon on the status bar. You can activate this mode in multiple ways. You can set it from the "Do Not Disturb" submenu in the device settings or from its card in the Control Center.

## Low Power Mode:

A very useful tool that can be used to extend the battery life on your device is the "Low Power Mode" setting. You can convert the phone into power saving mode by going into 'Settings", under the "Battery" submenu. This will help you in various ways to use your phone longer and conserve battery life. You can also see the App utilization from the bar above and close Apps that are using more space and battery to maximize battery life.

## Screenshot:

Screenshots can be useful for capturing your screen as an image, without having to take a physical photograph of your device. To do this, hold the side button and the top volume button at the same time.

## Tap to Top:

When going through long notes and documents, going back at the top can seem like a time-consuming and frustrating hassle. In order to save yourself from that, just tap the very top of your iPhone's screen and it will take you back to the very first page of the document.

## Quickly Add Symbols:

In order to help you use your new device to its full functionality, there are many tools within its programming to streamline its use. The keyboard, for example, has a shortcut to add symbols quickly without forcing the user to scroll through multiple specialized keyboards. You can tap and hold certain keys within the device's keyboard in order to pull up various symbols and characters that would otherwise require several steps to use.

## Customized Auto-Correct:

The iPhone's operating system, iOS, is quick at guessing what you might want to type next. In order to customize your text patterns and mannerisms, this predictive text feature can be useful. In order to manage this feature, you can go to your device's general settings, scroll down and tap Keyboard. Select Text Replacement and you will see what text replacements you currently have set up.

## Rich Formatting:

Rich formatting is a handy trick to make certain parts of your App's texts stand out and be different. Click open a rich formatting App, select the text that you want to edit by tapping it twice and choose the formatting menu.

## Speak Selection:

You can have your iPhone XS read out your texts by simply enabling speak selection. To do this, go into 'General Settings' and choose the 'Accessibility' option. Select 'Speak Selection' from there. Once you do this, you will be able to find the option to 'Speak' in your messages by long pressing it.

## Saved Information:

In order to save time in filling the same account information again and again, you can make your iPhone memorize the details so when it is time to input the data, your iPhone auto fills the required information. Just go to the device settings and select "Autofill" under the "Safari" submenu.

## Customized Message Replies to Missed Calls:

You can easily customize replies and keep them for the calls that you are unable to answer. This is handy when you don't have time to type a message. These messages can be set under the "Phone settings, in the "Respond With Text" Submenu.

## Call Reminders:

You can set your iPhone to remind you to make calls at certain times, in case you miss a call or have one scheduled. This can be accomplished from the "Reminders" Application on the home screen. If you are unable to receive a call when it comes in, you can tap the "Remind Me" button to set the reminder for a specific time.

## Customize Animoji:

Customized animoji can be set up with the help of the facial recognition tool. The system recognizes your facial expressions in the front camera. Simply pull up the App drawer in the message App, swipe toward the right, and select the animoji icon. This icon will resemble the monkey emoji. Then swipe right until you see the new memoji icon, which will resemble a plus symbol. This allows the user to customize their memoji as they like. After you are finished, tap the "Done" button at the top of the screen to save your memoji and use them in your iMessages.

## Video Recording:

You can record videos on your iPhone by using the "Camera" application. This can be accessed from the home screen, or from the control center if you have its card enabled. You can also set the camera to record higher resolution videos by going into the settings, under "Photos & Camera". You can then scroll down and select the "Camera" submenu and tap "Record Video" to change the resolution.

## Taking Photos While Recording:

The amazing possibility of taking pictures while shooting a video is what makes shooting fun and easy. In order to take a photo, simply hit the small photo icon that on your device's display, while still continuing to hold the record button for your video. This will decrease the quality of the images, but not to an extreme degree.

## YouTube Zoom:

In order to take full advantage of large HD displays, Apple added a feature where you can zoom into the YouTube video to spread them over the landscape display canvas by merely pinching into the screen.

## Customized Music Timer:

There is a timer on the Music App in the iPhone XS. You might want to go to sleep while listening to music and, while at it, your phone will be playing songs throughout the night. This can run your battery down, heavily. You can turn on the timer and set the time by which you would like the music to stop. Open the Clock App's timer tab. Select how long you want your timer to last for and then press 'When Timer Ends.' Select 'Stop Playing' from the bottom of the menu. Tap 'start' on the timer and continue listening to the music using the Music App. The music will automatically stop playing when the timer ends. This technique also works on audio books and other types of media.

## Siri Activation:

Activating Siri on the iPhone models of the XS, XS Max, and XR can be somewhat different when compared to their earlier models. This is because of the exclusion of a physical home button. With the new digital home bar, accomplishing simple tasks is now a little bit different, as several of these gestures have had to be remapped to new ones that accommodate this new setup. Luckily, the new commands for these services are just as simple as before. To activate Siri, for example, utilizes the few Face ID, gesture controls, and the hold button on the right side of the iPhone. To activate Siri, you simply need to press and hold the hold button on the right side of the device. After a brief moment, Siri will open and pop up. If Type to Siri is enabled, the device's keyboard will also open, allowing you to type to talk to Siri, as opposed to speaking out loud. You can also, if this feature is enabled, tap the dictation button on your keyboard to speak audibly to communicate with Siri as well. Additionally, you can take this another step further and simply say aloud, "Hey, Siri" in order to activate Siri. This is useful for moments when you may not want to spend time pushing the physical buttons on your phone, as well.

## Apple Pay:

Apple Pay is another useful feature that can help to streamline your day-to-day dealings. With it, you can connect your bank account and use your iPhone at any accepting point of service in place of your card. This way, you don't need to rifle through your wallet to make a payment, you can simply pull up your iPhone. To instantly open up the Apple Pay application, you can tap the hold button on the right side of the device two times.

This will open the application quickly and allow you to make these payments more easily than ever before.

## Child-Friendly Mode:

In order to save your new device from being misused or destroyed by children, the iPhone has a child-friendly option. To activate this mode, you simply need to go to the "Restrictions" section of your device's general settings. From there, you can limit access to specified apps, block in-app purchases, and set an age range for appropriate content as you deem necessary.

# Conclusion

The latest iPhone models are some of the most advanced smartphones available on the market today. They had already generated a significant amount of hype and anticipation even before their official launch, and despite their high price, they are on their way to becoming one of the bestselling smartphones of 2019.

Apple will also benefit from launching three variations at different price points in order to help in diversifying its product reach. The new models look beautiful and are all much-valued upgrades to the previous model, the iPhone X, which has been discontinued with the release of the XS, XS Max, and XR.

The new iPhones have larger battery capacities which help to make them even more 'mobile' than previous versions and help them to stand out above other competing devices. Thanks to a fast processor, high RAM, top-of-the-line screen resolution, and many more amazing and impressive features, these models are equally great for professional use, recreation, and even for artistic uses and content creation. The handfuls of novel features in these new models can make their use smoother and more enjoyable, as well as simply streamlining day-to-day life and adding ease to all types of interactions one might encounter. These features can sometimes be confusing, irritating, and sometimes even difficult to understand and use effectively, but hopefully, this book has helped you to gain the tools necessary to do so and gain the most out of your new iPhone and all of its incredibly versatile features.

# Description

The iPhone family of products has been known since its initial release of the original iPhone all the way back in 2007. Over the course of the 11 years since the release of the original iPhone and its operating system, the iPhone OS (or iOS) 1.0, there have been a number of advancements and improvements to the technology and designs of these products that have managed to keep the iPhone consistently at the top of the smartphone market since they released.

With all of these improvements to the iPhones over the years, it can be difficult and even seemingly impossible for us to keep track of all of these complicated devices' incredibly broad features and capabilities. The newest additions to apple's very large family of products are the successors to the iPhone X. The iPhone XS, iPhone XS Max, and iPhone XR are packed with useful tools to help you to get the most use out of your phone that you can. The handfuls of novel features in these new devices can make their use smoother and more enjoyable, as well as simply streamlining day-to-day life and adding an astonishing sense of ease to all types of interactions one might find themselves in.

These features can sometimes be confusing, irritating, and even difficult to understand and use effectively.

The Handy Guide For Your iPhone XS, XS Max, and XR is designed to help you to gain all of the tools necessary to understand all of these various features and gain the most out of your new iPhone and all of its incredibly versatile features. This book is meant to illuminate the features of these new devices and their operating system, the iPhone Operating System (or iOS), in great detail. It will include their specifications, pros and cons, tips and tricks to help you use them to their best and fullest capacity, and a clear and differential analysis of the latest products in comparison to their ancestors. By the end, you should possess all of the tools necessary to do so and properly utilize all of the applications and various other features available to you on your new iPhone XS, XS Max, or XR.

## Links to Pictures

https://pixabay.com/en/icon-icons-computer-phoneapple-1971130/

https://pixabay.com/en/technology-iphone-x-iphonephone-3068617/

https://pixabay.com/en/iphone-smartphone-appsapple-inc-410311/

https://pixabay.com/en/iphone-x-iphone-x-applemobile-3566142/

https://pixabay.com/en/iphone-x-iphone-x-applemobile-3501731/

https://pixabay.com/en/iphone-ios-apple-6s-pluswhite-1067988/

https://pixabay.com/en/iphone-x-samsung-galaxys8-2957216/

https://pixabay.com/en/smartphone-cellphone-applei-phone-1894723/

https://pixabay.com/en/apple-concert-dark-iphonelights-1836071/

https://pixabay.com/en/conference-workshopiphone-3677032/

https://cdn.pixabay.com/photo/2018/01/11/21/27/desk-3076954_1280.jpg

https://cdn.pixabay.com/photo/2016/12/01/18/17/mobile-phone-1875813_1280.jpg

https://cdn.pixabay.com/photo/2016/11/29/05/08/apple-1867461_1280.jpg

https://cdn.pixabay.com/photo/2017/10/12/22/17/business-2846221_1280.jpg

https://cdn.pixabay.com/photo/2018/03/09/19/36/iphone-x-3212446_1280.jpg

https://cdn.pixabay.com/photo/2018/06/28/11/37/iphone-3503673_1280.jpg

https://cdn.pixabay.com/photo/2017/12/21/20/56/phone-3032551_1280.jpg

https://cdn.pixabay.com/photo/2019/03/06/10/51/iphone-x-4038013_1280.jpg

https://cdn.pixabay.com/photo/2017/12/25/20/14/iphone-3039062_1280.jpg

https://cdn.pixabay.com/photo/2018/06/29/14/03/iphone-3506067_1280.jpg

.

www.ingramcontent.com/pod-product-compliance
Lightning Source LLC
Chambersburg PA
CBHW020709180526

45163CB00008B/3010